Rugby Union
RULES

Rugby Union

RULES

EDDIE KNIGHTS

WARD LOCK

A WARD LOCK BOOK

First published in the UK 1997
by Ward Lock
Wellington House, 125 Strand,
London WC2R 0BB

A Cassell Imprint

Distributed in the United States
by Sterling Publishing Co., Inc.
387 Park Avenue South, New York,
NY 10016–8810

A British Library Cataloguing in Publication
Data block for this book may be obtained from
the British Library

ISBN 0 7063 7559 9

Photographs by Colorsport

Typeset by Business Color Print, Welshpool,
Powys, Wales

Printed and bound in Great Britain by
The Bath Press

Frontispiece Despite French attempts to
thwart him, an England forward takes a clean
catch in the line-out in a 1996 Five Nations
Championship match.

CONTENTS

INTRODUCTION

When learning to drive a car you must eventually pass a test to prove you know how to control the vehicle and can use it within the laws of motoring. In short, the test establishes whether you are ready to join the ranks of properly qualified motorists. This is not the case in sport for, while every junior or novice player may receive some guidance or already have some knowledge of the rules, participants are usually expected to learn as they go along, and they are certainly not precluded from playing until they can prove they know the laws. Some will still be learning the rules of their sport on the day they retire!

Does this matter? Yes, it does, and for several reasons. First, the player who is ignorant of the laws is often the one who questions the officials first, fails to understand certain rulings and is a disruptive influence. Secondly, someone who transgresses the rules invariably gives his opponents the advantage – a foolish and unpopular

way of playing the game. Thirdly, team sport cannot be played without controls, and these are usually exercised by unpaid, volunteer officials, who deserve the support of every player. Lastly, to win within the rules is so much more satisfying than believing you can, or have to, flout them in order to succeed.

The aim of this book is to explain the rules of Rugby Union as they will be encountered by players, coaches and spectators. Legalistic terms and expressions have been dispensed with so as to make the text more readable, but anyone who wants to take the game seriously and gain the fullest understanding of it is urged to consult the official rule book and its regular amendments. Most rugby matches are competitive but take place outside high-profile league or cup organization and control. The text will concentrate, therefore, on those matters essential to the smooth running of the game at this more common, amateur level.

Of the many international team sports, rugby is one that is enjoying one of the fastest growths of players and spectators. This is the case at all levels, in all age groups and in countries that have learnt the game only recently. There are several reasons to explain the sport's mounting popularity:

- it can be played outdoors on a simple pitch without expensive equipment
- it allows body contact but throws up fewer disputes than many that do not
- it is an all-action game that is enjoyable to participate in and watch
- it offers a role to all physiques – small and large, fast and slow
- its infinite variety of tactical and positional moves means that every match offers fresh dimensions for players and spectators

That it can boast these benefits is due, in part, to its longstanding and strict adherence to the laws of the game and its severe censure of those who do not abide by them.

With new nations coming to the sport every year it is important that those controlling this expansion, and taking part in it, obtain an early appreciation of the game's regulations. In this way growth can be channelled down the healthy, successful path that rugby has followed in past decades. Etiquette, fairness and good sense are all features from which the toughest team sport can benefit.

● NOTE

This book uses the male gender throughout in the interests of readability. This should not be taken for ignorance of the very strong growth in women's rugby, which both author and publisher wish to support and encourage.

CONVERSION TABLE

1 millimetre (mm)	= 0.03 inch
1 centimetre (cm)	= 0.93 inch
1 metre (m)	= 1.09 yards, 3.28 feet
1 kilometre (km)	= 0.62 mile
1 gram (g)	= 0.03 ounce
1 kilogram (kg)	= 2.20 pounds
6.35 kilograms	= 1 stone

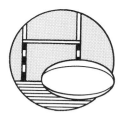

BEFORE YOU START

● THE GROUND

The pitch markings are shown on the diagram on the right. The laws stipulate maximum width and length measurements but do not set minimums; it is acknowledged that pitches of smaller dimensions can stage matches, especially for youth games.

The field-of-play is within the touch- and goal-lines, as will be shown by the rulings on touch and try scoring (see pages 21 and 24).

The surface must be covered with grass or another suitable material, and while the referee has responsibility to check pitch markings and ground conditions, the visiting team must

Thomas Castaignede kicks off from the halfway line to start the France v. Ireland game in the 1996 Five Nations Championship.

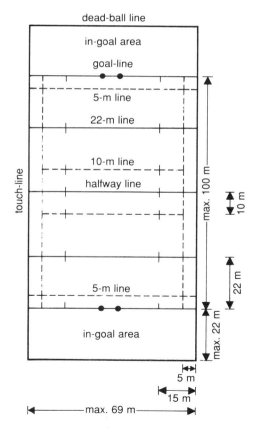

The pitch markings and the key measurements.

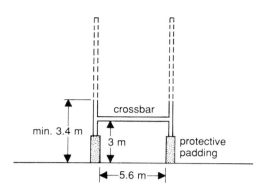

The goal-posts and their dimensions.

It may be that both teams will accept one or more of these shortcomings in order to avoid undue delay to the match, but player safety and the removal of causes of dispute must be treated seriously. If the match is delayed while such matters are attended to, the required standard must be agreed. It may not be possible to correct fully all faults in time, and one must bear in mind the repercussions of the delay, for example, deteriorating light.

make any objection to the official before the kick-off. Look out for these common faults:

- goalposts not perpendicular
- goalposts not adequately padded at their base
- flags missing, of incorrect height or badly positioned
- pitch markings incomplete or unclear

● THE BALL

The four-panelled ball should be of the dimensions shown in the diagram and should have a pressure of 0.67–0.70 kg per sq cm at the start of the game. If a ball needs to be replaced during the

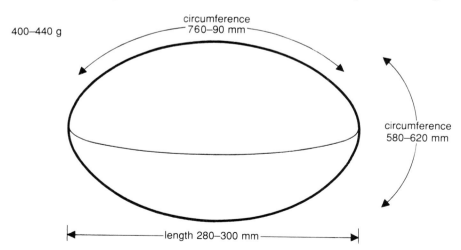

The ball, showing correct dimensions.

match, it should be of an identical standard, if possible, and referees must not allow a team to gain advantage by changing the ball without good cause.

Smaller balls are available for junior matches.

● NUMBER OF PLAYERS

Rugby Union is played between teams of fifteen players. The number of players allowed to be substituted depends on the nature of the game and the local rules governing it. For matches played outside league or other competitive conditions, the team officials and the referee should set replacement limits for the game. Below the senior leagues it is unlikely that medical advice can be obtained about the nature of a player's injury; in such circumstances the referee must assess the validity of an injury and agree to the subsequent replacement.

Recent rulings have allowed tactical substitutions to be undertaken without justification on medical grounds.

● PLAYING KIT

Players must not wear items that could cause injury to themselves or others.

Thus:

- rings, bracelets and the like must be removed or taped over
- boot studs must conform to accepted standards, be circular and firmly fixed. Official measurements are – maximum length from sole: 18 mm; diameter at top: 10 mm; at base: 13 mm. Studs that develop rough or scarred edges must be effectively repaired or replaced
- shoulder pads or other supportive clothing that includes hard or reinforced material cannot be worn

The referee can decide before or during the match that a player's kit is dangerous and insist on its repair or removal. That player must leave the field of play to effect the remedy if the game is in progress.

It is preferable that the two teams wear shorts and socks of different colour/pattern; the referee should wear colours that are wholly different from those of the two teams.

● THE TOSS AND TIMING OF THE MATCH

Adult matches are usually of 80 minutes' duration with two equal halves divided by an interval of no more than five minutes, during which the teams change ends. Youth and junior matches may be played over a shorter time (see page 67).

Stoppages in play, such as for injuries, lengthy ball retrieval or unfair delay by players, will be noted by the referee and be made up by the addition of the lost time at the end of the half in question. The referee should ensure all parties know the playing time before kick-off.

The referee will call the captains together before the start of play to toss a coin for choice of ends or kick-off.

Nick Farr-Jones (Australia) and Finlay Calder (British Lions) toss for kick-off before the third test in 1989.

OFFICIALS

● REFEREE

It should go without saying that every match should be controlled by a referee and that his status and the decisions he makes should be respected and accepted by players, team officials and supporters. Rugby Union has an enviable reputation for player discipline that has been built up over many years. The high standards of past generations partly account for this, as does the severe treatment meted out to anyone who has failed to meet them.

Ideally the referee should not be associated with either of the teams represented, though this cannot always be the case in the lower leagues and at school and junior level. Whatever his position before and after the game, the nominated official should take his role seriously and fulfil it as efficiently as he can. Among items on his checklist before the start of the match will be:

- to have a thorough and up-to-date knowledge of the laws
- to be aware of any special rules affecting the game, for example agreed number of substitutes
- to check the pitch for poor or incorrect markings, dangerous obstacles, and its general suitability for play
- to ensure both teams are ready to start on time and that they are wearing correct kit (see page 11)
- to see that two touch judges are available and to assess their level of expertise
- to possess a personal kit including a watch – preferably two, of which one will be a stopwatch – pen and paper, whistle, and red and yellow cards, if appropriate

The referee is sole arbiter of the timing of the match and its score, though he may enlist the back-up of his touch judges on timing and find the score is being posted on a board at the ground. If he notices the latter is incorrect he should ask for it to be changed.

By blowing his whistle the referee indicates the start, stoppage or restart, and end of play. He will whistle for the stoppage of play when:

- the ball has been grounded in the in-goal area
- the ball has gone out of play
- he awards a penalty kick, free kick, fair catch or scrummage
- the ball is unplayable or to continue play would be dangerous, for example in a collapsed scrum, or when the pitch is invaded
- a player is injured and the ball next becomes dead, although he may stop play immediately on noticing an injury that he judges to be very serious
- the ball touches him and one team gains an advantage, in which case a scrummage is awarded, with the team that last played the ball having the put-in

The referee blows for half time and full time when the allotted period, including any allowance for temporary stoppages, has expired and the ball is dead. If the ball is in play when time expires, the whistle should be blown when the ball next goes dead unless this has been brought about by a try or a fair catch, in which case the next kick is allowed and the play stopped when the conversion is completed or the ball next goes dead.

The referee's whistle signals the commencement of play at:

- the start of play and the resumption after the interval
- the resumption of play after a try or its conversion attempt
- the resumption after another score, for example penalty kick or drop goal

The referee controls the movement on and off the pitch of trainers, coaches and medical advisers, injured players and substitutes. Players who leave the pitch for treatment to an injury must obtain the referee's permission to return; on sustaining an open, bleeding wound a player must leave the field immediately and, should he return, satisfy the referee that the injury has been securely dressed. Injured players can be substituted by a temporary replacement who will become permanent if the injured player cannot return.

For referee signals, see page 68.

● TOUCH JUDGES

Normally each team provides a touch judge. He will patrol the whole length of one side of the pitch and leave the side-line only when called upon to take position behind the posts to adjudicate on the success or otherwise of a kick at goal. He should carry a flag, or a similar item, and indicate his decisions with it.

A test for the touch judge. If the ball is caught and the feet stay inside the line, the ball is not in touch.

therefore, from which the resultant throw-in should be taken. He will indicate the team awarded the throw-in by pointing with his arm to the end of the field they are defending. The touch judge lowers his flag once play has been restarted except when he has noted an infringement at the throw, namely, the thrower putting a foot into the field-of-play, an advantage being gained at a quick throw-in by use of a replacement ball, or the wrong team taking the throw. In such instances he

Assuming the player grounds the ball correctly, a try is awarded if he does so before any part of his body makes contact with the touch-line or beyond. Even though his tackler might be in touch and still holding him, this does not necessarily mean that the ball carrier is in touch.

The touch judge is under the direction and control of the referee at all times; the latter has the power to override the decisions of a touch judge or even have him replaced when faced with poor performance or misconduct.

The principal task for the touch judge is to indicate when the ball or a player carrying it has gone into touch or into touch-in-goal. He must stand, with flag raised, at the point which the ball has gone out of play and, will raise his flag in front of him to indicate to the referee that he has seen the incident.

For gauging the line, and successful completion, of a place kick at goal, each judge must take up position behind a post and raise his flag to indicate success if he sees the ball pass inside the post. Kicks passing above the height of the post but within an imaginary extension of it are deemed successful; kicks that rebound from the uprights or the crossbar but still drop between them are also fair.

It is unusual in amateur and youth matches for the touch judge to signal incidents of foul play to the referee – as might be the case in higher-grade matches, where all three officials are likely to have refereeing qualifications. If the referee expects such support to be given he should ensure the touch judges are aware of this before the start of play.

Remember: the referee cannot alter his decision once taken, except when it is made before he sees a touch judge's signal or receives a report from his colleague under Law 26 (Misconduct or Dangerous Play). It is officially against the law for him to change his mind. So not only is it unwise to argue because it will incur a penalty, it is also a waste of time.

● TEAM MANAGEMENT

Managers, coaches, physiotherapists and medical advisers are not allowed on to the pitch without the agreement of the referee, except at the half-time interval where their attendance must not be allowed to extend the break. When they are on the pitch to treat an injured player they will be permitted only up to one minute to assess and treat, unless there are special circumstances such as obvious serious injury or there is a delay in being able safely to move the injured player.

In park matches where coaches and supporters are close to the sideline, and not held back by a barrier, they must avoid encroaching on to the field-of-play or obstructing the view of the touch judge. If such transgressions persist, the referee is entitled to take whatever action he feels is required to keep that area clear and safe.

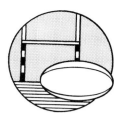

STARTING AND RESTARTING

● KICK-OFF

The game is started by a place kick taken from the centre of the halfway line by a player from the team awarded that kick as a result of winning the toss. A kick from the same position begins the second half, taken by the team that received the kick which started the game and restarts the game after a successful kick or conversion.

The ball must cross the opponents' 10-m line in the air or on the ground. If

Positions at the kick-off. The team taking the kick must be behind the halfway line, the receiving team behind their 10-metre line, and the ball must reach that mark for play to continue.

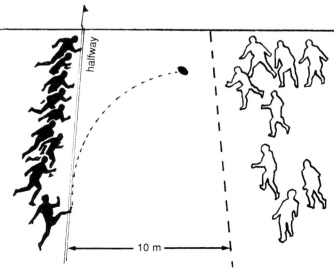

Previous pages Stewart Campbell and Bob Wainwright of Scotland vie to take a catch from England's kick-off in the 1996 Five Nations Championship.

it does not then the receiving team are given the put-in to a scrummage from where the kick was taken, or may opt to have the kick taken again. Should the ball go directly into touch on either side of the 10-m line without being touched by a player from either side, the same options are available to the receiving side.

Should the kick-off travel as far as the goal-line of the receiving team without being touched, they may play the ball, ground it or immediately kick it dead. If they make the ball dead they can opt for a scrummage at the halfway line or have the kick taken again, but they must have made the move to kick the ball dead without delay; it is not permissible to attempt to play the ball and then have second thoughts.

All the players from the team taking the kick-off must be behind the ball when it is kicked; if they are not then a scrummage is awarded to the receiving team. The receiving team must be behind their ten-metre line when the kick is taken; if they are not, and gain advantage, the kick is taken again.

The restart from a 22-m drop-out. The defending team must stay behind the kicker and the line.

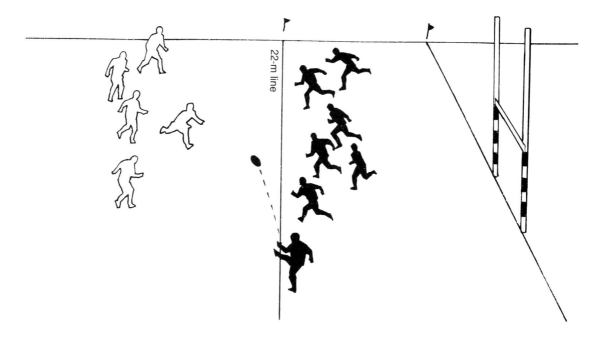

22-m line

SCORES AND SCORING

The means by which points are scored are:

- a try – 5 points
- a penalty try – 5 points
- converting a try into a goal – 2 points
- a goal from a penalty kick – 3 points
- a dropped goal from open play – 3 points

 TRY

Tries are scored by grounding the ball in the in-goal area of the opposing team. The ball can enter the in-goal area carried by an attacker or by a member of the defending side, or in the air or on the ground with players in pursuit.

The attacking player carrying the ball needs only to ground it within the marked area; if he is chasing the ball he has to exert downward pressure on it within the in-goal area before an opponent can. In cases where a player from the defending team carries the ball into the in-goal area but then loses control of it before grounding it, if he fails to pick it up cleanly or to ground it correctly, then an attacking player can score a try by being the first to ground the ball. A further complication here can be when a defending player seeking to play the ball in his in-goal area is tackled and prevented from correctly grounding the ball by that tackle, for example by the tackler holding him off the ground. In this situation the player must release the ball. If none of his team-mates is close by, his tackler or another opponent can touch the ball down to score.

To correctly ground the ball being carried it needs only to be touched to the turf; the rolling ball must be pressed down with the hand or arm or can be fallen on, to create downward pressure. Beware of being too casual: most rugby players or spectators can remember cursing the 'showboater' who, at the end of an easy overlap, a mazy run or a long chase, decides on some extravagant gesture to confirm his score. He can often do just the opposite, by sowing seeds of doubt in the referee's mind. Remember, it is the official who adjudicates on the fair grounding of a ball for a score; if a graceful but purposeless salmon leap across the line causes him to question whether the ball was perhaps dropped on to the ground, five or seven points may have been sacrificed along with the good will of fourteen colleagues.

There can be times when a mêlée of players near the goal-line prevents the referee being sure a try has been correctly scored. He is not allowed to guess, assume or expect the ball has been grounded – he has to see it happen. Even if his positioning might be questioned it is his decision that is final and he cannot award a try unless he can *see* the hand, arm or body of an attacker ground it. He does not have to know which player scored the try, provided he is certain it was a player from the attacking side. At a scrum, ruck or maul close to the goal-line all eight forwards, or a good number of them, might fall on the ball once it

England's Will Carling scores a try in the corner against Wales in a 1990 international. For such a try to be legal the feet must be in the field-of-play when the ball is grounded.

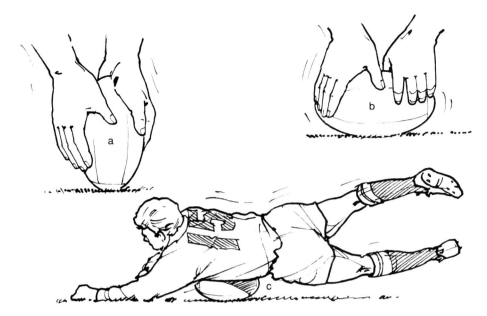

Scoring the try by:
a) placing the ball on the ground;
b) exerting downward pressure on the rolling or stationary ball;
c) diving on the ball.

reaches the in-goal area, and provided he is sure no opposing player was within reach of the ball, the referee will award the try – even if he is unsure of the identity of the actual scorer. This emphasizes the need for opposing teams to wear clothing of contrasting colours and patterns (see page 11).

Remember: because the goal-line is part of the in-goal area, the ball grounded on the line constitutes a fair score; this does not apply to the touch-in-goal or dead-ball lines.

Most tries are scored without dispute, with the player carrying the

ball clearly grounding it correctly. In the case of a race between attacking and defending players, chasing the lofted or rolling ball, the referee will look for the first hand or arm to exert downward force to the ball on the ground. The pushover try is usually clear enough; if it is not, no try is awarded.

Disputes do arise, however, when players are tackled short of the line but still manage to ground the ball on or behind the line. If the ball carrier is tackled but his momentum sees him reach the line, and he there grounds the ball, then a try can be awarded – assuming he has retained control of the ball – even if the ball has come into contact with the ground in the tackle. Also, if the ball carrier is tackled short of the line but immediately

reaches forward to ground the ball on or behind the line then this too will be given as a fair score. He breaks the law – as would be the case wherever the tackle is made – if he does not release the ball quickly; the laws allow him to 'put the ball on the ground in any direction . . . provided the action is immediate'. Hence, as the tackle is completed and the ball carrier is brought to the ground, he can reach forward to lay the ball on the ground, but he must do this in one movement; he must not adjust his position on the ground by pushing his body forward in a second motion. It is this extra movement that makes the attempt to score a try illegal.

A tackled player grounded short of the line can reach forward to place the ball on or beyond the line provided he does so immediately.

● PENALTY TRY

It is human nature to try and limit the scale of any loss. Hence, a defending team or one of its number may well choose to infringe the rules close to the try-line in the hope that, at worst, three points will be conceded for the resulting penalty rather than the five or seven that a try and conversion would score. The first aim of such tactics will be not to be found out at all, and an unobservant referee might well be fooled by the diverse schemes deployed.

To discourage such action referees are empowered to award a penalty try when they judge that foul play has been committed wilfully and prevented a try being scored. They may well choose to give a penalty kick at the first sign of such infringement, though they do not have to: they can wait to see evidence that the first instance was no accident before giving a penalty try. There can always be some doubt that a try would have been scored, but the referee is required to assess only that a very good chance has been denied by the foul. His decision will be shown by him running to the goal-line between the posts and indicating a try; the conversion is taken from a line through

England's Will Carling eludes a tackle near the touch-line and heads for the corner flag to score against Wales in a 1990 international.

this point, making a seven-point score almost inevitable.

Common examples of illegal moves producing a penalty try are when a defending pack constantly collapses a scrum close to their line to prevent a pushover try or clean possession to their opponents, or allows its forwards in the same location to widen the scrummages, once formed, so as to discourage try-scoring runs around the formation by the back row or scrum-half. Defending players seeking to stop a try-scoring run may persistently move offside or tackle illegally – high or by tripping – and if, in the opinion of the referee, this prevents a score he can award a penalty try. Such decisions need not be on plays close to the goal-line; a penalty try can be given if a clear breakaway, perhaps from an interception far downfield, is stopped by the last defender tripping the runner with his foot.

● CONVERTING A TRY

Grounding the ball on or behind the opponents' goal-line enables a team to attempt to convert the points that have been gained into a larger total by taking a kick at the goal.

Anyone on the team can take the kick, but all other players must be behind him; the opposition must be behind the goal-line until the kicker begins his run-up, at which time they can silently charge forward in an attempt to block the kick or distract the player.

The kick is taken from any distance the kicker chooses on a line through the point where the ball was grounded for the try. The referee will mark this point when he indicates the try, and the player selected to kick the conversion must ensure he places the ball on a line from that mark and parallel to the touch-line. The distance he places the ball from the goal-line is at his discretion but is normally the point that gives him the best angle at least distance, taking into account the strength of the wind and his own level of ability and technique. Most kickers feel they can kick longer and more accurately from a place kick but a try can be converted by a drop kick if preferred.

The kicker will be allowed reasonable time to tee the ball on the ground and prepare to take the kick. It is, unfortunately, in vogue for players to take an undue amount of time to wipe their boots, hands and even their nose, toss a blade of grass into the air, straighten their hair and pose for the crowd. It can only be hoped that this trend is discouraged before it has to be legislated against. The referee can add time on if he so chooses, but he seldom seems to.

If the ball falls over before the kicker begins his run-up the referee will allow it to be repositioned, but if this happens during the kicker's approach then he must continue with the kick even if the ball is rolling. In strong

The conversion kick. The opposing team can rush the kicker from their position behind the goal-line, but must do so in silence.

winds the kicker might select to have a team-mate hold the ball steady. This must be done with the ball resting on the ground and stopped from falling by one finger or a hand.

The team defending a conversion must not advance until the kicker begins his run-up; if they do the kick can be retaken if it fails. If the players charge the kick down and have moved legally then the kick fails, though it is possible for it to be deflected over the crossbar by a charging player, in which case it is successful.

The scoring of a try means a team may attempt the conversion kick, but they do not have to. If the wind is so fierce as to make a successful kick unlikely or if the team requires as much time as possible to score a further try to win the game, then the right to take the kick can be forfeited. When the scores are close at the end of the game a captain should always be aware of the ratio of points available to time taken, whether he is winning or losing.

● PENALTY GOAL KICK

As with the conversion of a try, the penalty goal kick can be attempted as a drop kick, but if this ever used it is usually for reasons of speed, and it is more likely to be taken as a place kick.

Depending on the weather and ground conditions and the ability of the kicker, the kick might be taken from inside the opponents' 22-m line or well back, even beyond the halfway line on occasions. A captain may ask his kicker to attempt a long penalty goal kick, even when the odds are against success, if this takes time off the clock towards the end of a game that he is winning and/or if it forces the opposition to play the ball close to their own line.

Defenders are not allowed to charge a penalty kick but need stand only ten metres away rather than behind the goal-line. If a defending player does move while the kick is being taken and does so in a manner that the referee believes may have affected the kicker, the kick can be retaken. Furthermore, the ball remains in play until either the kick is successful, the ball goes dead or is grounded by the defending team in their in-goal area. So the kicking team will have its fastest runners pursue the attempt at goal with the view of putting defenders under pressure when the ball lands. The ball can also rebound from the posts, or a defensive kick to touch fail badly, and fresh attacking options open up as a result.

England's Jonathan Webb attempts to convert a try against France in the 1991 Rugby World Cup quarter-final. Note that the opposition must stand behind the goal-line, but can charge towards the ball as the kicker's run-up commences.

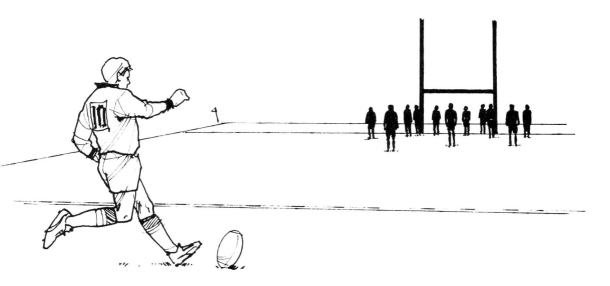

Team-mates chasing the kick must be behind the kicker until he strikes the ball but thereafter they can tackle any player who catches the ball, and prepare for any move should the defending team choose to play the ball once it is collected.

If the ball falls short of the goal-line defenders have no option; if it runs into the in-goal area they can ground it and restart with a drop kick from their 22-m line. Otherwise they can choose to run with the ball or run forward into a better position to clear to touch with a punt.

Rob Andrew of Wasps kicking a penalty goal against Bristol in 1995. Note that the opposing team need only be 10m back but the players are not allowed to charge as the kick is being taken.

The penalty kick. The opposing team need not retire behind the goal-line, but must stand still while the kick is being taken.

Once a team has decided to try for a penalty goal from an awarded kick, and indicated this to the referee, they cannot change their mind. The referee will signal the touch judges to take up position behind the posts and a fair attempt at kicking the goal must be made.

The team that has conceded the penalty should not assume an attempt will be made to kick a goal; if they turn their backs on the play, an alert opposition can gain advantage by taking a tap kick and running with the ball, which they are entitled to do until they have told the official they are kicking for goal.

● DROPPED GOAL

The special skill required to kick a dropped goal successfully when under the pressure of a competitive game is not bestowed on many. Even those who have mastered the art will not expect a strike rate much higher than 25 per cent until they match the right moment to try the kick to their skill level. Having said this, a gambler would probably take three points once in four attempts rather than go all-out for the five-point try, bearing in mind the number of moves that reach the opponent's 22-m line but do not get converted into tries.

The ball must be kicked on or after the first bounce – in practical terms, on the half-volley. It can be deflected over the bar by an opposing player's attempted block, but if it strikes a team-mate of the kicker the referee will blow for accidental offside unless the defending team take advantage of the loose ball.

Several circumstances make a dropped-goal attempt likely: when half-backs are faced with tight marking close to the scrum and along the backs; after a series of failed attempts to score a try and when the captain does not want to lose the attacking position without scoring some points; or when any player receives a short clearance and finds himself in space but without support to start an attacking move.

The player who can return a better strike rate than that mentioned above is a fine asset to a team provided his decision-making is sound. A fly-half, for example, must know when to sacrifice a three-quarter move in favour of a dropped-goal effort, and not give away the chance of five or seven points without good cause. A back who averages one dropped goal a match through the season is almost certainly to be valued; but this rule of thumb is rendered invalid if he needs a dozen attempts every game to achieve that return.

Remember: you cannot score from a free kick. It is permissible, however, to tap a free kick to one of your colleagues, who can then attempt a dropped goal.

PASSING AND CATCHING THE BALL

You must pass backwards to go forward! The cardinal rule of Rugby Union is that you can only move the ball forward by running with it or kicking it – you cannot throw it forward. Because this is an absolute and basic tenet of the game it has to be enforced stringently, otherwise it becomes eroded and abused. Therefore, a ball that is passed forward at the narrowest of angles or knocked forward one inch by hand without being held under control breaks the rules. Harsh it may be, but it must be; consider the alternative to test the purpose of the rule.

When the ball is thrown from the hand in open play it must travel along or behind an invisible line parallel to the goal-lines. If the ball is passed level between two players running forward at pace, it is, strictly speaking, bound to actually travel forward, but the referee will usually be satisfied if the receiving player is behind the team-mate passing the ball.

If your pass travels backwards but then bounces ahead of the 'invisible line' on hitting the ground, it is fair; the same applies to a long pass that starts correctly but is blown forward by the wind. Less clear-cut is a long throw delivered with spin which starts on an acceptable line but then curves forward. Ultimately, it is the official who is there to judge such difficult questions and it is he you have to satisfy.

When a ball is literally handed to the next player it still constitutes a pass, so the receiving player must be behind the player in possession if he is not to be judged offside. In such a case a scrum is the correct decision, unless the referee determines the illegal pass was a deliberate ploy, in which case he is able to award a penalty kick.

If a player throws a ball forward into space, whether or not it is because he believes a team-mate is there, the referee may award a free kick if he believes it to have been intentional.

A knock-on can happen only from the hands or arms and even then it will not be called if the player recovers control of the ball before it hits the ground. Most games will produce an example of a player fumbling a ball and the referee putting the whistle to his lips only for the player eventually to grasp hold of the ball and continue the move. A knock-on is not called if a player charging down an opponent's kick is struck by the ball on the hands or arms and sees it fall in front of him. Play is stopped only if he has had time to try to catch and control the ball in the act of charging the kick down and fails to do so, knocking it forward in the process.

If the ball is directed forward by any other part of the body – head, chest,

No knock-on. When the ball is knocked forward by a player intercepting a kick, a knock-on is not awarded.

thigh, knee – it is not judged a knock-on unless it also hits the hands or arms. The ball that falls backwards, after a fumble when taking a pass or fielding a kick, is not a knock-on.

Catching an ovoid rugby ball is seldom easy. Unless it is efficiently thrown, even a short pass can have the ball arriving at the receiver toppling end over end – hence the need to exert some spin on the ball on every pass you make. Moreover, a high punt rarely arrives at the catcher in a smooth trajectory that would make it as easy to grasp as a round ball.

The rugby player seeking to catch a high ball is not especially well protected by the laws. He can call for a fair catch (a 'mark') and so give himself time to clear the ball without pressure (it is considered dangerous play if a catcher is tackled while in the air jumping to field the ball). Otherwise he has to keep his eye on the ball and look to gather it cleanly even if he knows, and can probably hear, that half a dozen opposing players are charging after the dropping ball, and him. A 'mark' can only be claimed when the player:

- has at least one foot on the ground
- fields the ball cleanly and securely from an opposition punt
- is on or behind his own 22-m line
- shouts 'mark' clearly enough for the referee to hear

The catcher should not, in such circumstances, assume that the 'mark' will be awarded and should be ready

In this 1993 international, France's Philippe Saint-André leaps ahead of England's Jon Webb to take a catch in open play.

Calling for the mark. The player catching the ball must have one foot firmly on the ground and make an audible call for the 'mark'.

to play the ball if it is not. The player will often find it difficult to judge himself whether he has met the criteria above; the referee may have players between himself and the catcher, and so not *see* the catch, and in the hurly-burly of a match, he might not hear the call . . . especially if it is followed by a yelp as the catcher is tackled.

Once the mark is awarded the opposing players cannot move beyond that point. The catcher can then retreat the few yards necessary to kick for touch safely and without hindrance.

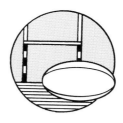

THE SCRUMMAGE

It is not for this book to adjudicate on whether the scrummage is the best means of returning the ball to play after it has become unplayable or when a minor breach of rules has occurred. Will it forever be an integral part of the game, or might it be one of the first amendments to be made as the game is played by more countries or, perhaps, merges with the Rugby League code in some way? For the present it is a major tactical feature of the sport, which is codified in one of the more complex rules in the book – Law 20 – and which is more open to abuse and misdemeanour than most other aspects.

The front row, with the hooker flanked by two prop forwards, showing how they bind together.

● POSITIONING AND STRUCTURE OF THE SCRUM

The basis of the scrummage is the front row of players – the hooker in the centre and the two prop forwards – and the two who 'lock' into the spaces created by the front trio. No scrum can proceed until this quintet is in place; they are the minimum required to form a scrummage.

In normal circumstances a scrum is formed where the incident or unplayable ball position occurred; it is *always* started from the mark made by the referee when awarding it. He may choose to move it away from the touch-line if the actual mark is too close to allow the scrum to function properly; if the mark is near to the goal-line he must start it from a point where the front five of the defending team can stand in the field of play.

The front row is the foundation around which the rest of the scrum is formed. The three players must link together as shown in the diagram opposite and interlock their heads with the opposing front three. The prop forward whose head is free at the end of the line of six when interlocked is termed the 'loose-head' prop, and it is on his side that his scrum-half will put the ball in – because it means that the hooker of that team is closer to the ball.

The six players of the two front rows, when interlocked, create the tunnel into which the ball is rolled so that it can be hooked back on its way into play. The front row players must be in a position to push forward at all times, that is, with their feet on the ground and the loose-head player only holding his opponent with his arm inside that player's right arm; it will help his forward push but does the same for his opponent. A front-row player must not pull an opponent down, take his own feet off the ground or twist his own body downwards with the intention of collapsing the scrum; it is dangerous – especially in junior rugby – and illegal. To secure the ball from their own put-in or to disrupt their opponents from doing the same, the front row have only one tactic: to push as hard as they can.

Prior to the put-in, a tunnel is created by the two front rows of the scrum.

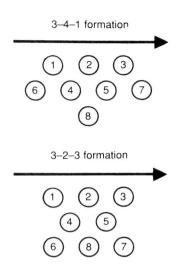

3–4–1 formation

3–2–3 formation

The two most popular scrummage formations.

The second row – the locks – must bind together and position themselves between their three front players. They are bound by the same rules that apply to the front row and their role is also to push, especially to generate the second drive forward as a shock move to ensure possession or deny it to the opposition. The second row can be of four players if the flankers – numbers 7 and 9 – choose to bind to the locks rather than the number 8. Provided the front row remains at three, there is no limit to the numbers or formation of the scrum, though the normal structure is 3–2–3 or 3–4–1.

In this 1992 France v. Scotland international, the French scrum-half, Fabien Galthie, watches the packs engage and prepares to put the ball in.

The flankers are the flair players of the scrum. If they bind to the scrum at its formation they can move clear, for defensive or offensive reasons, as the scrummage progresses. In this respect the law is being changed, but they cannot adjust their position outwards while still bound to the scrum if the purpose is to obstruct an opponent who makes a run around the formation.

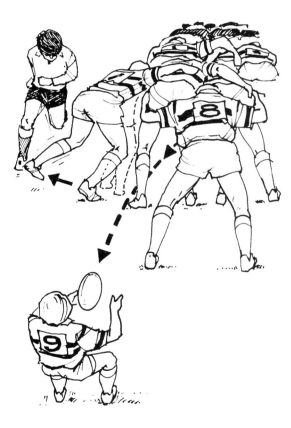

Illegal expansion of the width of the scrum in order to block opposition moves.

If the structure of the scrummage fails – when the front rows do not interlock properly, or the formation collapses, or a player is lifted off his feet – the referee will halt play immediately and call for the scrum to reset.

Only the prop forward can hold an opponent in a scrummage with his outer arm. A clandestine move by a flanker to grab at an opposing forward and affect his impact on the drive forward is against the rules but can sometimes be missed by a referee who does not regularly alternate his position at such set plays.

Where the forwards are evenly matched a pack will often do little to secure possession from a scrum when their opponents have the put-in; why expend effort and energy when the odds are so stacked against you and you are unlikely to win the ball? Some packs will in such circumstances use the sudden push. This shock tactic stands a better chance of success. The forwards will often simply stand their ground and be ready to break quickly once the ball is out. It is in this situation where forwards can be at their most devious because they are not having to concentrate on pushing. The referee will look for the front row trying to obstruct the tunnel, collapse the scrum or twist sideways rather than forwards – any move to disrupt the possession of their opponents, delay the exit of the ball from the scrummage or use up the energy of opposing players.

How the prop forwards should engage. These are the only forwards in the scrum who can lock arms with the opposition.

● THE PUT-IN: WHO GETS IT?

We have all heard players complaining and spectators catcalling when the put-in to a scrum is awarded, in their view, to the wrong side. This usually stems from an ignorance of the rules, though it is not beyond the bounds of possibility that the referee may have misread the play or failed to see a knock-on.

In general terms, the team not responsible for the stoppage of play is awarded the scrum. This is clear enough when a player knocks-on or throws a forward pass: his opponents put the ball into the ensuing scrummage. If, however, the scrum is given because the ball has become unplayable beneath a mass of hot, sweaty bodies reluctant to release it, and no offence has been committed, the team moving forward before everything stopped will get the put-in. This can cause consternation when an attacking move travels 50 metres or so before it is halted and the defenders manage to carry the ball a metre forward as they stem the flow; the latter will get the scrum. If the referee judges that no side had the momentum, he will award the scrum to the team in the attacking position. This rule has the advantage of encouraging a defending team to do more than simply 'kill' the ball; if they manage to repel the attack by the smallest of forward surges they get a better chance to clear their lines.

Even though the side who was moving forward gets the scrummage after a ruck, the team that carries the ball into the maul, and then fails to recycle it, loses the put-in. This rule, which is sometimes difficult to interpret in the frenzy of a match, exists to stop the kind of negative play whereby a team might keep forming almost static mauls with no ambition to free the ball. Before the rules were changed, teams used this tactic to run time off the clock when it suited them. If a kick ahead into open play is caught by a player who is then enveloped by a static maul before he can move forward, any scrum that follows will go to the team whose player fielded the ball.

At a scrum that forms after an injury stoppage, the team that last had possession will have the put-in.

● THE PUT-IN: HOW IT MUST BE DONE

No attempt to hook the ball can be made before the ball hits the ground from the scrum-half's feed; the hooker cannot stretch his leg forward before the ball is delivered and the scrum-half cannot throw it on to that leg to deflect it back through the scrum. He must feed the ball straight into the tunnel formed by the front rows.

The scrum-half will develop some audible signal to his front row so that the attempt to hook the ball can be made simultaneously with the put-in. The movement should be smooth,

The scrum-half cannot take the ball from the position in diagram (a) because it is still 'in' the formation. The number 8 must walk over the ball or heel to the scrum-half (b).

The put-in to two packs in the 3–4–1 formation.

quick and efficient if the action is synchronized – and the referee will be satisfied. If the calling is inaccurate and the ball arrives before the hooker expects it, it may pass straight through the tunnel and the whole process has to be started again; if the ball arrives after the hooker has raised his foot in readiness then he will be penalized and his team will lose the chance of the put-in.

The route of the ball out of the scrum can be by any path provided it exits behind the front foot of the prop. It is deemed to be out of the scrum once it is clear of the boundary of the formation, that is (assuming the whole pack forms the scrum) usually when the ball passes the rear foot of the flanker or the number 8. If, however, any members of the back row disengage before the ball reaches them, they have, by separating, reduced its size and can pick up the ball even though it is in front of them.

Any member of the front row may hook at the ball to direct it backwards, but no player is the scrummage can handle the ball while it is being heeled, except when the pack is attempting a 'pushover' try. A scrum-half cannot pick the ball out from between the legs of his forwards – he has to wait for it to pass the feet of the players at the perimeter of the formation.

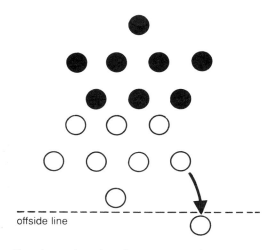

If a player detaches from a scrum, he must retreat behind the feet of the last man.

● OFFSIDE AT THE SCRUMMAGE

There are two offside lines at the scrummage: for the scrum-half it is a line through the ball wherever it is; for the backs it is the rear feet of their side of the scrum.

The scrum-half who feeds in the ball can take up any position around the formation while he waits for the ball to

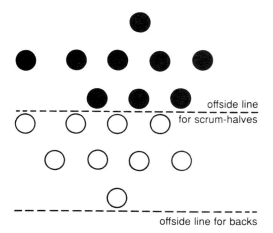

The offside lines at a set scrum.

be heeled, provided he remains behind the ball. His opposite number must remain on the other side – onside – of the ball and can only move around the side of the scrum into which the ball was fed. If he is seeking to disrupt the handling and passing of the ball by his opposing forwards or scrum-half he will edge around the unit as the ball is routed backwards. In doing so he can get on the wrong side of the ball if the heel is slower than he expects or he loses sight of it. If he influences play from such a position, by intercepting the ball, tackling his opposite number or gaining advantage in pursuit of the ball, then the referee will penalize him. Remember, the pack receiving the put-in cannot expand its shape widthwise once it has engaged, so the opposing scrum-half can follow the ball as it is heeled and then dive to tackle the number 9 from an onside position, and therefore legally, provided he has stayed behind the ball.

The offside line at scrummages for other players is the back feet of the formation, usually the number 8. And not only must the backs stay behind that point but so too any forwards who detach during the heel. If, for example, a flanker disengages but the number 8 stays in position, he must not delay in getting behind that team-mate; if the whole of the back row detaches, the feet of the lock forwards become the offside line. The law is due for change in respect of detaching from the scrum.

● THE TURNING SCRUM

In recent years the referee has been required to call for a scrum to be restarted if it turns beyond 90 degrees before the ball exits. This rule has helped to clarify the offside questions that arose in the past when the wheeling scrum saw the ball coming back into play with most parties being in a position that could be considered offside. Now the scrummage is started again, from the same position as when the whistle was first blown. A pack that continually turns the scrum in this manner is using unfair play and will be penalized, but it is still a legitimate tactic. Defending forwards have the chance to direct their push at various angles in an attempt to disrupt the feed.

In such situations scrum-halves must continue to stay behind the ball and the three-quarters must be behind the back foot of the forward nearest to their own line. This, as the scrum wheels, may become someone other than the number 8.

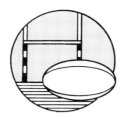

RUCKS AND MAULS

A ruck is formed when the ball is on the ground – in the muck – and players from each team are on their feet and in physical contact around it; a maul is formed when players from each team are in physical contact around a player holding the ball.

The early stages of a ruck. The ball is on the ground and will now be heeled back to the scrum-half.

● THE RUCK

Where two or three are gathered together – and the ball is on the ground – you have a ruck. But these two or three must be bound together with an arm interlocked for them to be deemed part of the ruck. This is important as the feet of the last player

in the ruck mark the offside line, and if that person is merely standing with his hand resting on his team-mate in front of him then he is not part of the ruck. The offside line will be through the nearest fullybound player.

You can join a ruck only alongside or behind the hindmost player in the formation, not in front of him, but once you are part of it the penalties you might incur are mostly as for a set scrum. You cannot handle the ball unless you are attempting to score a try and you must keep on your feet. If you deliberately collapse the ruck and do so regularly you can be penalized.

If the ruck becomes stationary and the ball shows no sign of being returned to open play, the referee will

As England's Will Carling attemps to fend off a tackle in a 1990 international against Wales, team-mates behind prepare to lend support. It is in such situations that mauls are formed.

award a scrummage to the team moving forward most recently before the whistle was blown. He will allow time for the ball to be won after the ruck is created but will not allow it to remain static for long – better to call for a set scrum that will ensure the ball is freed.

As with a scrummage, the purpose of a ruck is to recycle the ball, so if you prevent it happening, or it doesn't happen quickly enough, action has to be taken.

● THE MAUL

The ball carrier and two other players make a maul. The player with the ball is held by an opponent without being brought to ground, so a colleague comes to his assistance – the maul begins. Soon other offensive players join the throng, with the aim of transferring the ball from the carrier back into free play or adding weight to the forward impetus, or, if from the defending team, stopping the drive or trying to wrestle the ball free.

As with the ruck, the offside line is taken from the feet of the last player who is genuinely bound into the formation. However, since the maul is more likely to be on the move, with players spinning out of the unit and rejoining it, the temptation is far greater to come into the group from the side, that is, from an offside position. This is especially true for the defending side, for players forced out of a retreating maul that they want to

In this 1995 England v. France international, England players Leonard, Bracken and Moore tie in the ball in a rolling maul.

rejoin. Not only do they have to run to the back of the formation, but the effort is doubled because of having to 'overtake' the players being pushed backwards. On the other side, the pack moving forward can spill players to each side knowing that they can more easily turn on to the back player and keep the momentum going.

Once a player goes to ground in a maul the rest often follow, the ball often becomes unplayable and the referee will call for a scrum, having allowed a short time to establish whether the ball is available or not. If the player has deliberately fallen on or

The beginnings of a maul. The ball carrier is stopped, so a supporting player binds on to him to add forward thrust or help feed the ball backwards.

around the ball to prevent it being won, a penalty will be given.

Remember: the onus is on the team carrying the ball into the maul to free it into open play within reasonable time. If the maul grinds to a halt and the ball does not emerge, the put-in to the awarded scrum will go *against* the team that was in possession when the maul began.

LINE-OUTS

When the ball goes into touch legally – that is, it is not part of an infringement such as kicking the ball directly into touch from outside the 22-m line, or immediately preceded by an infringement, then a line-out is called. It sounds a simple enough process for returning the ball to the field of play, but in practice it is fraught with clandestine tactical deviance. In addition, the relevant rule, Law 23, presents referees with endless problems of interpretation.

true, because it is taken from the mark on the line indicated by the touch judge, and he does not always get it right! If the ball has been kicked out on the full by a player outside his 22-m

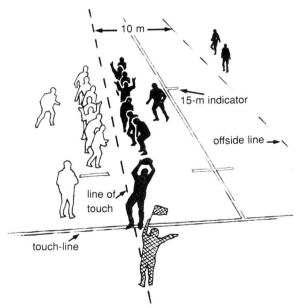

The line-out positions. The two sets of opposing players must be 5m away from the touch-line and 1m apart.

● POSITION OF THE THROW

Unless a team chooses to take a quick throw (see page 52), the ball is thrown in from the position on the touch-line that it crossed when passing from the field-of-play. Actually this is not strictly

line, the throw will be taken from a point level with his position when he kicked.

The two sets of forwards, or as many of them as the throwing team nominates, then take up position either side of an imaginary line at right angles to the touch judge's mark.

a) A line-out formation showing some of the many ways in which the laws can be broken. **b)** the correct formation.

● THE LINE-OUT FORMATION

At least two players from each team must line up for a throw-in. The team awarded the throw decides how many players will form the line, usually the full pack minus the player taking the throw. The opposing team must match this number.

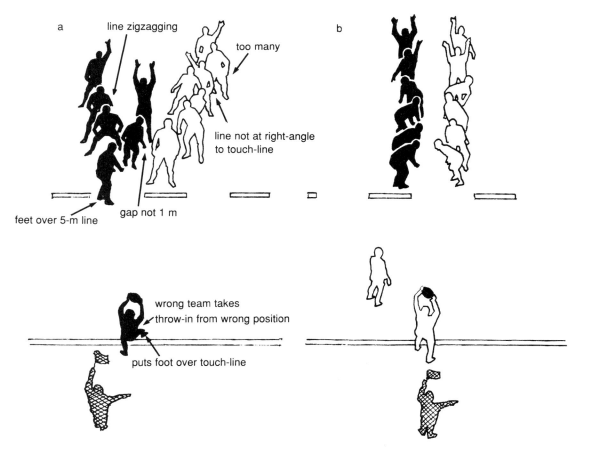

a
line zigzagging
too many
line not at right-angle to touch-line
feet over 5-m line
gap not 1 m

b

wrong team takes throw-in from wrong position
puts foot over touch-line

The line-out can be manned from the 5-m line – the dotted line parallel to the touch-line – to a point 15m from touch. The front player need not stand at the 5-m line but if he does not his opposite number can still do so. Players who stand outside this 10-m space are not part of the line-out and are therefore not counted as members of it. Forwards who are not required at the line-out when it is shortened must retire to a point 10m from the line of the throw.

Until the ball is in the air and players begin to jump for it the two lines of players must be a metre apart, each of them half a metre to their side of the throwing line, taken from the touch judge. Entering this corridor before the ball is thrown is a free-kick offence.

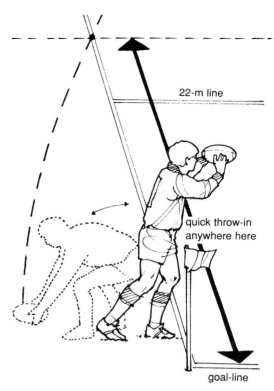

22-m line

quick throw-in anywhere here

goal-line

The throw-in can be taken from any position between where the ball crossed the line and the goal-line of the team that will take the throw, so long as the same ball is used and it has been retrieved by the thrower.

● THE THROW ITSELF

To return the ball to play by way of a throw-in does not actually require a full line-out formation and it need not be taken from the point where the ball crossed the line. If time allows, a team with the right to take the throw can do so from any point closer to their own goal-line from where it went out of play. The player taking the throw need not even throw it to a colleague; he could, if he thought it safe, throw the ball straight in-field, beyond the 5-m line, then run to it, collect it and play on. It is more likely that he will see a team-mate in line and throw it to him, but the rules do not discourage the quick throw-in option. Indeed it can be an effective riposte to the team that continually kicks long to keep the ball in their opponents' half; the quick throw-in, taken before the team has followed up on the kick, can begin a running counter-attack with the necessary space for it to be developed.

The danger in this ploy is all too obvious: a hurried throw, a lack of control, a missed pass, slowness in supporting play – and the advantage is lost.

The quick throw-in option cannot be used if the ball has been retrieved by anyone other than the thrower, or if a different ball is used to the one that has been kicked out of play. If such an attempt is made the referee will call for the throw to be retaken.

All throw-ins have to be thrown straight, travel at least 5m and be thrown by a player whose feet are outside the field of play. The throw does not have to be made by the hooker (though it often is), can be thrown under- or overarm and can be projected beyond 15m provided it stays straight. Though it is absolutely sensible to have one player specialize in taking throw-ins and probably best

if this a forward, it is somewhat ironic that most teams now use the hooker, often the smallest pack member. While you will want to keep your tallest players for jumping, it is worth bearing in mind that the taller the thrower the easier it is for him to throw the ball at pace on a trajectory that bypasses the front jumpers and reaches the middle or the back of the line without interception.

● LINE-OUT OFFENCES

There are many ways to become offside at the line-out, but it should be easy enough to stay onside if you keep your wits about you.

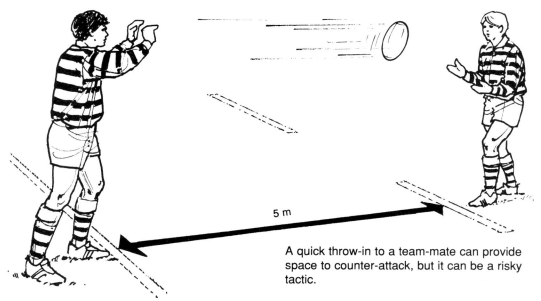

5 m

A quick throw-in to a team-mate can provide space to counter-attack, but it can be a risky tactic.

The offside line at the throw is the imaginary line between the two sets of forwards indicated by the position of the touch judge. As the ball is thrown and in play it is that line that marks offside; if or when a ruck or maul develops then the offside rules for those moves apply. If you move offside a penalty is given. Offside is also given if you break from the formation or move beyond the 15-m line before the ball is delivered; the same applies if you are not called to join the line-out but do not retire 10m back. Once the ball is thrown you must not get in front of it except in the process of jumping, when, if you do not collect it, you must quickly get back onside.

In the frenzy of jumping for the ball the referee has to watch for the offence of barging. Two men jumping in competition with each other will inevitably collide, but if one hurls himself into his opponent without making a genuine attempt for the ball, simply to disrupt the catch of the opposing player, the referee will penalize him for barging. The devious line-out man can make a blatant leap into a jumper from the other team look like a proper challenge, so the official will be watchful for the repeat offender. Once a player is in mid-air, jumping for the ball and about to catch it, he is very susceptible to a hefty nudge.

Wales's Derwyn Jones soars to take a clean catch in the line-out in a Five Nations Championship match against England, which took place in 1996.

Faced with such trickery many referees now turn a blind eye to the 'support' given to the main jumper by team-mates. You are not allowed to lift a colleague (Law 23.15c), and that same rule bans 'support to enable him to jump'. The referee will blow quickly if he sees a player hoisted by another, but if a player gets airborne by himself and then finds himself almost sitting on the backs and shoulders of team-mates wedged underneath him the official may let play continue.

The jumper must not improve his leap by levering himself up on an opponent alongside. If he did so with his inside arm he could only attempt to palm the ball away with his other, and this too is illegal; you must only use your inside arm to deflect the ball if you are not able to catch the ball with both hands. If you reach up with both arms but the ball deflects off your outside arm, the referee will probably give you the benefit of the doubt.

Just as you must not tackle the player jumping to catch the ball in open play, so in the line-out you must not tackle, pull or push the body of a player who is in mid-leap.

Remember: the throw must reach the 5-m line, and if a player darts

Illegal line-out moves:
a) the jumper is being lifted by a team-mate;
b) the jumper is levering himself up on an opponent and using his outside arm to deflect the ball.

a

b

Illegal line-out move. The ball must travel 5m.

the same, before lunging forward to take the short throw.

In the mêlée of a line-out it is very easy for the pack that finds itself winning the ball to stand stiffly in position, perhaps with arms spread a little wider than is truly necessary to secure their balance, and so prevent the opposition from getting past to challenge the player in possession. Being obstruction this is against the rules, but in practice only the most obvious examples get penalized. The forward who stands four-square, protecting his scrum-half but not physically holding back an opponent with his arms, will seldom be thought to infringe . . . and three or four forwards creating such a barrier are difficult to penetrate.

forward to claim it before it has travelled that distance, the referee can penalize him by awarding a free kick. If the player at the front of the line is planning such a move he should edge backwards, hoping his marker will do

Illegal line-out move. A player is deliberately blocking opponents trying to get to the ball.

If a long throw is attempted neither the players in the line-out or those outside it can move towards the ball until it is in the air.

When the ball is in the air it is then open season for all players, forwards and backs, to run to where the ball will fall. The throw still has to be straight, however, and that is a rarity when a rugby ball is propelled over such a distance.

Most of the misdemeanours at line-outs are punished by free-kick awards, but barging, levering and obstruction are penalty-kick offences – as is offside in all its guises.

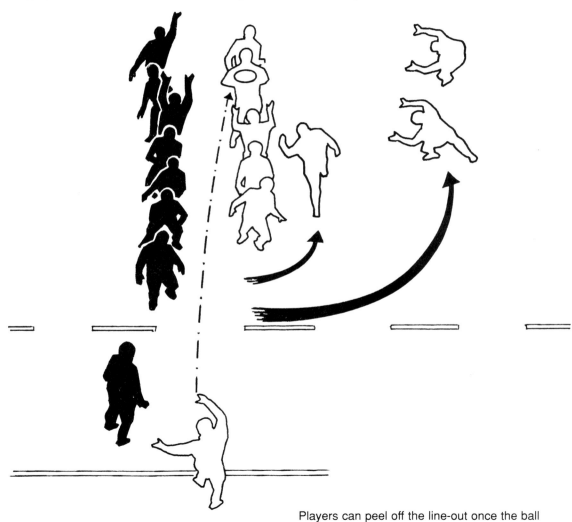

Players can peel off the line-out once the ball is thrown.

MISUNDERSTANDINGS AND CONFUSIONS

● OFFSIDE AT RUCKS AND MAULS

We have dealt with offside lines and positions as we have covered the different sectors of the game, but it does no harm to repeat some of the laws; the whistle for an offside decision is the one greeted with the most derision and with the least understanding.

The first rule is that you can only be offside in open play if you are in front of the ball carrier or the man who played it last. Unfortunately, there are also some exceptions.

The offside situation in general play. A kicks the ball. As B moves to catch it, C, D and E are all offside. D and E are more than 10m away from B and would not be penalized. C is closer and a penalty would be awarded if he made any move towards the ball.

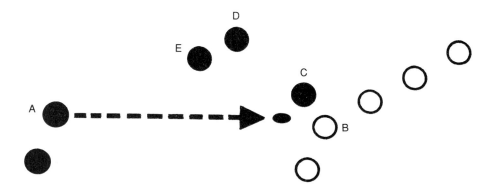

When a ruck or maul becomes established a player can often find himself on the wrong side, often by quite some way if a long kick or a fast-running movement has taken place. As he trundles back to an onside position he can be offside if the opponents win the ball and start attacking. He can do nothing to redeem his situation until the opposing team has run 5m or kicked the ball, after which he can involve himself again. The player who is slow around the pitch is penalized but this does encourage a faster game.

● ACCIDENTAL OFFSIDE

A good deal of Rugby Union football is left to the referee's discretion or interpretation, and here is an example. If a player knows he is in an offside position and raises his hands in acknowledgement as the game carries on around him, is he offside – albeit accidentally – if one of his players running with the ball bumps into him? And what happens if a kick forward cannons into him while he is standing offside? The answer is that 'play

a) Long kick ahead.
b) Attacking players pursue, hold the catcher and secure possession.
c) Slow forwards from the defending team involve themselves in the game from the 'wrong side'.

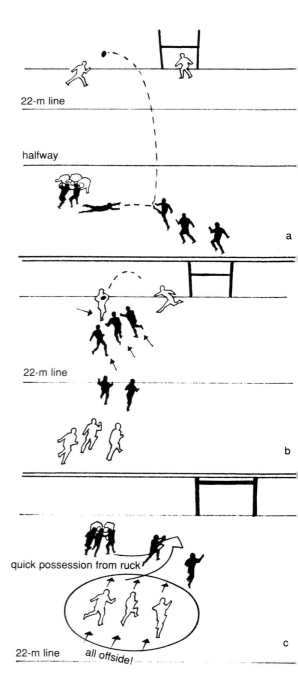

22-m line

halfway

a

22-m line

b

quick possession from ruck

22-m line   all offside!

c

should be allowed to continue' unless the offending player brings an advantage to his team by his position. Thus, if he innocently stands still, is cannoned into and his position prevents his opponents from getting in a clean tackle on the ball carrier, the referee will award a scrum to the opposing team, for accidental offside. Should the ball strike him while he is in an offside position but then rebound to an opponent who can then gain advantage, no whistle need be blown.

Some examples of accidental offside might be interpreted as obstruction if the referee believes the player, though feigning innocence, has deliberately placed himself where he will obstruct the opposition. A penalty kick would be awarded in this situation as the referee has judged it as unfair play.

● ADVANTAGE

The player who sees an offence committed and stands waiting for the whistle must rid himself of this dangerous habit. He must keep moving and watch for who is gaining advantage. If the team that has not broken the rules gains positional advantage and/or possession the referee may choose to let play proceed. Try not to be the player who stands hands held high for the referee's whistle when a pass from a team-mate on the counter-attack hits you in the midriff – as you glare at the man with the whistle, your colleagues will be looking hard at you.

Another occasion when you must not stop play, expecting the whistle, is if the ball or ball carrier strikes the referee. The official, not the player, decides whether a team has been disadvantaged and will only whistle if he believes this is the case. Some players will see the referee get in the way and complain when he allows play to continue, but the laws state that he should do this unless advantage has been gained by the opposing team. He may see players in positions that you, as a player, cannot and use that information to reach his snap decision.

● KICKING AFTER A 'MARK'

The player calling for a fair catch or 'mark' is required to take the resulting punt, be he a skilful kicker or a roughneck forward who has never practised the art. If he is injured as he takes the catch and cannot recover within one minute, the kick cannot be taken by a team-mate but a scrum is called at the point where the catch was taken and the put-in goes to the catcher's team.

If the player making the 'mark' is injured by an unfair challenge then a penalty will be awarded.

● UNFAIR TACKLES

Spectators cheer and colleagues yell support as a huge forward launches into an opposition back, heaves him off the ground and dumps him and the ball in the mud. Shame, because it is an unfair tackle and will not be allowed. Remember that you cannot tackle a player as he is in mid-air jumping to catch a ball, or use a foot to trip him up, or tackle high i.e. around the neck or with a stiff arm or late or early. Nor can you lift the player off the ground in the tackle, as there is a danger of his falling head first on to the ground.

The stiff-arm, high tackle is against the law.

It is illegal to tackle a player while he is in mid-air catching the ball.

To tackle the player before he has the ball is illegal.

● FREE KICK

The kick must be made with the foot or lower leg. It is common to see a player, seeking to take a quick tapped free kick to himself, touch the ball forward off his thigh or knee; this is against the rules. The ball must be propelled away from the mark, even if this is by tapping it a few inches into the hands or along the ground.

Ireland's David Humphreys delivers a crunching, but legal tackle on England's Phil de Glanville in a 1996 international.

● THE 10-METRE PENALTY

A referee is empowered to move a penalty or free-kick mark 10m forward if his decision is disputed by a player from the penalized team or if any of their players do not quickly retire 10m from the position of the kick. The referee does not carry a list of prohibited words so do not complain, answer back or question his authority; take your punishment. One referee may take a certain level of casual questioning and play on, while another

will take exception to any critical aside. A referee may even change his attitude during a match if he decides extra discipline is called for.

If a decision is genuinely not understood then the captain or pack leader should quietly seek clarification without delaying the game unduly; this is not a passport to complain, only to ask for a brief explanation . . . and accept it.

● INJURY TIME

It can be guaranteed that there will always be someone, in even the smallest of crowds, keeping a check on the time being played; it is also likely that one team will want the match to end and the other be happy for it to overrun.

No matter how many watches are being worn by members of the team management or the crowd, only one matters – the one worn by the referee and, maybe, those owned by the touch judges if they have been asked to assist the main official in timekeeping. But the referee is normally the sole arbiter of time; he alone can stop and start the watch. He is entitled to take into account the time taken to retrieve the ball, undue wasting of time by players, time taken to treat injured players and for physiotherapists to leave the pitch, and any excessive time taken in substituting players.

Indeed the factors involved in timekeeping are so various that you might just as well accept the referee's judgement.

● BLOCKING THE BALL

If you are tackled and become trapped with the ball under a few heavy forwards, or in some other way find yourself on the ground lying on or around the ball, it seems very unfair that you are expected to be able to move out of the way so that the ball can be played. Even experienced international players emerge from such pile-ups, having been penalized, shrugging their shoulders in disbelief. But life is cruel, and that is the law; if you are preventing the ball from being played a penalty kick can be awarded. If you don't like it, consider how easy it would be for you to make out that you had no alternative . . . the ball could be trapped for an eternity. So the law exists to combat negative or deceitful play, and you must release the ball and move away from it when tackled, and stay on your feet if you join a ruck – it will be a better game.

● BLIND REFEREES

This should go without saying, but it does no harm to spell it out again: play to the whistle. You may be absolutely certain you have seen the laws broken, but if the referee has not then you will not hear the whistle, and that can be embarrassing if you have stopped running. The fittest, fastest and most efficient referee can still miss a knock-on, or see it but view it differently from you; he may have half a dozen forwards between him and what you have seen clearly.

It is a cardinal sin for players to bear a grudge against a referee for a bad decision. It means that you lose concentration, running around the pitch waiting for what you will see as another lapse, when you should put such reversals behind you and get refocused on the game.

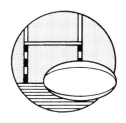

NEW LAWS, DIRECTIVES AND SPECIAL RULES

The rules of Rugby Union football are set by the International Rugby Football Board (IRB), which, at its regular meetings, formulates revisions and amendments to the rules, issues new laws and publishes directives. All players, coaches and referees should keep themselves informed about these changes, especially in view of the ground-breaking revolutions taking place in the game and the consequent likelihood of major alterations in the near future. The national boards and associations of the rugby-playing countries send delegates and observers to IRB meetings and will be able to answer any enquiries about the laws.

The move to making the game professional in some of the leading countries may not, in itself, change the rules of how the game is played, but the increased interest of the international media that will stem from this development might do so. One hopes that good sense will prevail and that the nature of the game will not be drastically changed and traditions forgotten on the whim of a television executive.

In the 1990s IRB directives affecting law interpretation have covered headgear and other protective clothing, and substitution. Revised laws are expected or planned for scrummage formation and execution.

The IRB also issues variations to the laws for use in youth matches and the seven-a-side game. The key amendments for youth games concern:

scrums
- there must be eight players on each side of the scrum or, in the event of injury or shortage of players, the packs must be of equal number

- all members of the scrummage must stay bound until the ball is out
- a scrum must not push forward more than 1.5 m or wheel more than 45 degrees
- if the first five players in a scrum present no contest to their opponents then the referee should allow uncontested scrummage, in which no forward push is permitted

dangerous play

- the employment of grouped runs from a tapped free kick close to the line and of 'flying wedge' formations in the same situation is banned

timing

- matches for under–19 competitions must not exceed 70 minutes of play; extra time must not be allowed, even in knockout competitions

substitutes

- players substituted because injury prevents them from continuing should not be allowed to return to the game

REFEREE SIGNALS

The correct signal, quickly and clearly given, can answer a question or quell dispute in an instant; unclear signals or none at all only exacerbate confusion, annoyance and argument. Whether a referee calls his decisions will be a matter of choice, but he should bear in mind that it is probably unwise to have players constantly turning to see a signal when an audible confirmation could help. Certainly the official should give audible instruction to players at points where they are waiting for his lead – at the scrummage when players should engage, at line-outs and kicks when they are in an incorrect position and at times when he is playing advantage (a short call to 'play on' will avoid problems). The signals fall into three categories:

- primary signals – which all officials should employ
- secondary signals – which clarify a decision and are therefore used by

diligent and efficient referees
- tertiary signals – which complement a referee's overall control of the game; they are used at his discretion, but can help players and spectators interpret his decisions

Primary signal: penalty kick.

Primary signal: free kick

Primary signal: try or penalty try.

Primary signal: advantage.

Secondary signal: scrummage awarded.

Secondary signal: forward pass or ball thrown forward (passing movement).

Secondary signal: knock-on (tap hands together).

Secondary signal: not releasing the ball.

Secondary signal: deliberately falling over or on to a player.

Secondary signal: diving to ground in close proximity to a tackle.

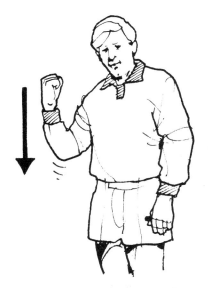

Secondary signal: pulling down (downward pulling movement).

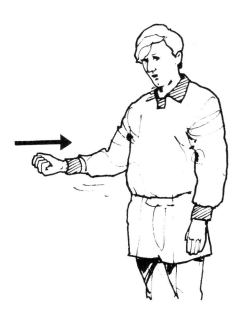

Secondary signal: pulling on (backwards pulling movement)

Secondary signal: scrum wheeling more than 90 degrees (rotate hand).

Secondary signal: foot up

Secondary signal: crooked put-in (demonstrate crooked delivery).

Secondary signal: improper binding (right hand on shoulder of outstretched left arm).

Secondary signal: deliberately collapsing ruck or maul (twisting downward movement with arms in front).

Secondary signal: handling on the ground
(backwards sweeping movement).

Secondary signal: using the outside arm at
the line-out.

Secondary signal: closing gap at line-out
(closing upstretched arms together).

Secondary signal: barging at the line-out.

Secondary signal: leaning on at the line-out (downward gesture).

Secondary signal: pushing at the line-out (pushing gesture).

Secondary signal: lifting at the line-out (lifting gesture).

Secondary signal: obstruction.

Secondary signal: offside at the line-out (move hand horizontally across chest).

Secondary signal: offside at ruck or maul – fringing (circle with finger pointing downwards).

Secondary signal: offside at ruck or maul – back foot (arm swinging in downward arc).

Secondary signal: offside at penalty or back of the scrum (arm up for penalty; other arm showing point of infringement).

Secondary signal: offside – remaining within 10m (circle hand above head).

Secondary signal: foul play – high tackle.

Secondary signal: use of the boot (stamping movement).

Secondary signal: foul play – punching (punch palm with fist).

Secondary signal: foul play – dissent (mimic jaw movement with hand)

Tertiary signal: award of a 22-m drop-out.

Tertiary signal: formation of a scrum.

Tertiary signal: 'stay on your feet' (upward movement of hands).

POSTSCRIPT

Like most team sports – American football, cricket, ice hockey – the game of rugby can appear complex and convoluted to the newcomer. In fact the laws of rugby are surprisingly brief when compared with apparently simple sports like golf, so it is really only the player and spectator who make the game complicated. When played fairly and with good spirit rugby is one of the most challenging yet rewarding sports; when played without due respect for the laws or watched in ignorance the pleasure can pall.

For those who play it, rugby is a fine combination of mental and physical ability; for those who watch it, it is a swift-moving pattern of graceful and astute ball skills. Whatever your purpose for gaining a greater knowledge of the rules of the game, may this book help you and your enthusiasm for the sport and, as a result, add to its increasing popularity.

INDEX

Page numbers in **bold** refer to the illustrations